First World War
and Army of Occupation
War Diary
France, Belgium and Germany

59 DIVISION
177 Infantry Brigade
Essex Regiment
15th Battalion
1 January 1918 - 31 August 1919

WO95/3023/5

The Naval & Military Press Ltd
www.nmarchive.com
Published in association with The National Archives

Published by

The Naval & Military Press Ltd

Unit 10 Ridgewood Industrial Park,

Uckfield, East Sussex,

TN22 5QE England

Tel: +44 (0) 1825 749494

www.naval-military-press.com

www.nmarchive.com

This diary has been reprinted in facsimile from the original. Any imperfections are inevitably reproduced and the quality may fall short of modern type and cartographic standards.

© **Crown Copyright**
Images reproduced by permission of The National Archives, London, England, 2015.

Contents

Document type	Place/Title	Date From	Date To
Heading	WO95/3023/6 15 Battalion Essex Regiment		
Heading	59th Division 177th Infy Bde 15th Bn. Essex Regt May 1918-Aug 1919. From U.k		
War Diary	St. Yammud	05/05/1918	05/05/1918
War Diary	Dover.	06/05/1918	06/05/1918
War Diary	Beaumaris.	07/05/1918	08/05/1918
War Diary	Marest	09/05/1918	09/05/1918
War Diary	Camp	10/05/1918	12/05/1918
War Diary	Grand Servins	01/06/1918	15/06/1918
War Diary	Le Vielfort	16/06/1918	17/06/1918
War Diary	Hestrus	18/06/1918	23/06/1918
War Diary	Coyecque	24/06/1918	09/07/1918
War Diary	Ambricourt	10/07/1918	31/07/1918
War Diary	Brettencourt	01/08/1918	02/08/1918
War Diary	Mercatel	03/08/1918	05/08/1918
War Diary	Chatmaigre	06/08/1918	08/08/1918
War Diary	Barly	09/08/1918	17/08/1918
War Diary	Brick Fields	18/08/1918	23/08/1918
War Diary	Saulty	24/08/1918	24/08/1918
War Diary	Lalacque	25/08/1918	26/08/1918
War Diary	St 7 Loris.	27/08/1918	31/08/1918
War Diary	Murillon	01/09/1918	02/09/1918
War Diary	Lestrem	03/09/1918	03/09/1918
War Diary	St Floris	04/09/1918	05/09/1918
War Diary	Epinette	06/09/1918	07/09/1918
War Diary	Lestrem	08/09/1918	09/09/1918
War Diary	L36 a75	10/09/1918	13/09/1918
War Diary	Mnd99	14/09/1918	16/09/1918
War Diary	Harleck Castle	17/09/1918	22/09/1918
War Diary	Riez Bailleul	23/09/1918	30/09/1918
War Diary	Fauquissart	01/10/1918	02/10/1918
War Diary	La Basse Road	03/10/1918	03/10/1918
War Diary	Laventie N Post	04/10/1918	05/10/1918
War Diary	Croix Marechal	06/10/1918	06/10/1918
War Diary	Front Line	07/10/1918	10/10/1918
War Diary	Fleurbaix	11/10/1918	16/10/1918
War Diary	Bois Grenier	17/10/1918	17/10/1918
War Diary	Premesques	18/10/1918	18/10/1918
War Diary	St. Maurice	19/10/1918	19/10/1918
War Diary	Lemarais	20/10/1918	20/10/1918
War Diary	Toufflers	21/10/1918	22/10/1918
War Diary	Hulans	23/10/1918	26/10/1918
War Diary	Epinette	27/10/1918	03/11/1918
War Diary	Hullans H20 d	04/11/1918	06/11/1918
War Diary	I9b 5.2 Do G23 B.	07/11/1918	08/11/1918
War Diary	Toufflers G 23 B	09/11/1918	10/11/1918
War Diary	Grand Rejet J7a	11/11/1918	11/11/1918
War Diary	Hullans H20d	12/11/1918	15/11/1918
War Diary	Gruson M33b	16/11/1918	16/11/1918
War Diary	Seclin V30a	17/11/1918	05/12/1918

War Diary	Noeux-Les-Mines K 18 B & d.	06/12/1918	31/12/1918
War Diary	Noeux-Les Mines K 24 b 8.7	01/01/1918	15/01/1918
War Diary	Martin Eglise	16/01/1919	26/02/1919
War Diary	Calais	27/02/1919	28/02/1919
Heading	War Diary Of 15th Battalion Essex Regiment For March, 1919.		
War Diary	Calais	01/03/1919	31/03/1919
Heading	15th Battn. Essex Regiment For April, 1919. Vol 12		
War Diary	Calais	01/04/1919	30/04/1919
Heading	War Diary Of 15th Battn. Essex Regiment For May, 1919. Vol 13		
War Diary	Calais	01/05/1919	31/05/1919
Heading	War Diary Of 15th Battn. Essex Regiment For June, 1919.		
War Diary	Calais	01/06/1919	30/06/1919
Heading	War Diary Of 15th Battn. Essex Regiment For July, 1919. Vol 15		
War Diary	Calais	01/07/1919	31/07/1919
Heading	War Diary Of 15th Battn. Essex Regt. For August, 1919. 177 Bde		
War Diary	Calais	01/08/1919	24/08/1919
War Diary	Beaumarais	25/08/1919	31/08/1919

WO95/3023/3a
5 Battalion Essex Regiment

59TH DIVISION
177TH INFY BDE

15TH BN ESSEX REGT
MAY 1918-AUG 1919.

From UK

CONFIDENTIAL

15TH G. Bn ESSEX REGT. WAR DIARY   MAY 1918.

INTELLIGENCE SUMMARY

Army Form C. 2118.

Place	Date	Hour	Summary of Events and Information	Remarks and references to Appendices
At Yarmouth	5/5/18	6 A.M.	The Battalion strength 33 Officers & 1062 Other Ranks, entrained Must Yarm Station in 3 Parties viz:— 1st Party 7.50 P. 2nd " 8.15 " morning, arriving, and moved to Lord Raglan Plymouth for Billets, respectively. 3rd Party leaving 6.50 pm same transport, entrained at 7mid 7am 10th it 11.30 am and arrived Dover Sp it 4 - 6 am	Gym
Dover	6/5/18	10am	Battalion embarked on 2 M. transports "S.S. ? & S.S. 10am and reached Calais & disembarked at 2 P—, and the attached A.M. 2 supplies kemp at BEAUMARIS arriving at 4.35 P.m.	Gym
Beaumaris	7/5/18	12 Noon	3 Officers and 14 Other Ranks proceeded in conference to ETAPLES	R.D.M.
Beaumaris	9/5/18	11am	Bn a Radn entrained at Fontinette Station CALAIS at 11 am and detrained at BRYAS at 8.30 P.m., & proceeded to Billets in GRIBOURT and MAREST	

L.R.

CONFIDENTIAL. 15th G Bn ESSEX REGT. WAR DIARY MAY 1918 CONTD. Army Form C. 2118.

INTELLIGENCE SUMMARY.

(Erase heading not required.)

Place	Date	Hour	Summary of Events and Information	Remarks and references to Appendices
MAREST	9/5/18	9a.m.	Battalion entrained at FAUX and proceeded to Camp at point outside GRAND SERVINS. Map Reference Sheet 36c Q.27.d.	8ms
CAMP	10/5/18		Erecting Tents & Bivouacs. Transport joined Battalion.	8ms
CAMP	11/5/18 a.m.		Commenced Digging B.R. Line Map Ref. Sheet 36.B. from point at M.4.b to point at Q.15.c.7.9	8ms
CAMP	12/5/18 & 13/5/18		Digging B.R. between daily. Platoon ordered by 147th Inf. Bdy. Horsing. From 6 to 16 hrs daily.	8ms

S.P. Cartwright
Lieut. Colonel,
Comdg 15th Bn. The Essex Regt. T.F.

CONFIDENTIAL

Army Form C. 2118.

WAR DIARY
~~INTELLIGENCE SUMMARY~~

(Erase heading not required.)   15TH G BN ESSEX REGT

June 1918

Instructions regarding War Diaries and Intelligence Summaries are contained in F. S. Regs., Part II. and the Staff Manual respectively. Title pages will be prepared in manuscript.

Place	Date	Hour	Summary of Events and Information	Remarks and references to Appendices
GRAND SERVINS	1 to 15	4.30-	DIGGING B.B. LINE	Sgn
LE VIEFORT	16	6.15 a.m	FINISHED WORK ON B.B. LINE PROCEEDED TO LE VIEFORT BY ROUTE MARCH AND CAMPED ONE NIGHT	MHQ Ref HB 4778 J ic 371 Sgn
LE VIEFORT	17	10 a.m	BN MOVED BY ROUTE MARCH TO HESTRUS	MOB REF HB 357 G 34 d Sgn
HESTRUS	18	6.45-	BN COMMENCED TRAINING	Sgn
HESTRUS	19	6.45 a.m 12.15	TRAINING	Sgn
do	20	6.45 a.m 12.15	do	nees
do	21	6.45 a.m 12.15	do DRAFT of 60 OR received from Base	nees
do	22	6.45 a.m 12.15	do	2 nees

Springfield Lt Col
Cmdg 15th Bn Essex Regt

CONFIDENTIAL.

WAR DIARY
or INTELLIGENCE SUMMARY.
1st G.B.n ESSEX REGT

JUNE 1918 (Contd)

Army Form C. 2118.

Place	Date	Hour	Summary of Events and Information	Remarks and references to Appendices
HESTRUS	23	10 a	BATTALION MOVED INTO BILLETS at COYECQUE - By ROUTE MARCH & F.W.d. - Move by Lorry to COYECQUE. MAP 44C	1st 2 Div P HNIE & ROS 5A 1pm - 9pm
COYECQUE	24	a.m	CONTINUED TRAINING	8am
Do	25	a.m	do	8am
Do	26	a.m	Training. Bn now designated 16 # 9 Bn Essex Regt	8am
Do	27	a.m	Training. 16 Bn & 13 Bn proceeded to Labour Coy BOULOGNE	8am
Do	28 to 30th	a.m	Training	8am

Bishop Croft
Lt Col
Comg 15 Garr Bn Essex Regt

CONFIDENTIAL.

Army Form C. 2118.

WAR DIARY

INTELLIGENCE SUMMARY

July 1918.

15th (S) Bn Essex Regt.

(Erase heading not required.)

Instructions regarding War Diaries and Intelligence Summaries are contained in F. S. Regs., Part II. and the Staff Manual respectively. Title pages will be prepared in manuscript.

Vol 3

Place	Date	Hour	Summary of Events and Information	Remarks and references to Appendices
COYECQUE	1	9 a.m.	Continued training	8mg
"	2	9 a.m.	" Training	8mg
"	3	9 a.m.	" Training	8mg
"	4	9 a.m.	" Training	8mg
"	5	9 a.m.	" Training	8mg
"	6	9 a.m.	" Training	8mg
"	7	9 a.m.	Moving about Bonds.	8mg
"	8	9 a.m.	Training	9mg

CONFIDENTIAL.

July 1918 Contd

Army Form C. 2118.

WAR DIARY
or
INTELLIGENCE SUMMARY.
(Erase heading not required.)

15th Bn Essex Regt.

Instructions regarding War Diaries and Intelligence Summaries are contained in F. S. Regs., Part II. and the Staff Manual respectively. Title pages will be prepared in manuscript.

Place	Date	Hour	Summary of Events and Information	Remarks and references to Appendices
COYECQUE	9	8 am	Bn proceeded by lorry to AMBRICOURT. MAP REF. LENS 11. 1/100000	8pm
AMBRICOURT	10	9 am	Continued training.	8pm
- do -	11, 12, 13th	9 am	"	8pm
- do -	14	9.55	Church Parade	8pm
- do -	15 to 20th	9 am	Continued training	8pm
- do -	21	10.15	Church Parade	8pm
- do -	22nd	9 am	Continued training	8pm
- do -	23rd	9 am	do do	8pm

S Moneypenny Lieut. Colonel,
Comdg 15th Bn. The Essex Regt.

Confidential   July 1918 Lond   Army Form C. 2118.

WAR DIARY
or
INTELLIGENCE SUMMARY
(Erase heading not required.)   15th Hre Essex Regt

Instructions regarding War Diaries and Intelligence Summaries are contained in F. S. Regs., Part II. and the Staff Manual respectively. Title pages will be prepared in manuscript.

Place	Date	Hour	Summary of Events and Information	Remarks and references to Appendices
AMBRICOURT	24	9 a.m.	Preparation for Move.	8 pm
"	25	2 p.m.	Bn moved by lorry to BRENTENCOURT. dep. LENS. II.	8 pm
"	26	9 a.m.	Training	8 pm
"	27	11.0 a.m.	Church Parade.	8 pm
"	28	9 a.m.	Training	8 pm
"	29	9 a.m.	do.	8 pm
"	30	9 a.m.	do	8 pm
"	31	9 a.m.	do	8 pm

S Murphy Major
Comg 15th Essex Regt

Original

CONFIDENTIAL

WAR DIARY
or
INTELLIGENCE SUMMARY.
(Erase heading not required.) 15TH BN ESSEX REGT.

AUGUST 1918.   Army Form C. 2118.

Place	Date	Hour	Summary of Events and Information	Remarks and references to Appendices
BRETTENCOURT	1/8/18	9 am	Training	8pm
"	2/8/18	9 pm	Battalion proceeded to take over left sub-sector front line. Map Ref M35 a 9.5.0 to M30 c 8.9.	Shelling 57th S.R. gas gas 5pm
"	3/9/18	daily	do	in trenches as above.	
MERCATEL	4/8/18	do	do	—	
"	5/8/18	10.8.	Relieved by 11th Bn L.L.R. + proceeded to CHAT MAIGRE. M27 a 3	Shelled 9pm 57th S.W.
CHAT MAIGRE	6/8/18	daily	in CHAT MAIGRE	9pm
do	8/8/18	do	do	9pm
do	9/8/18	10-30	Relieved by 2/5th Bn Kings Liverpool Regt + proceed to Berles.	9pm
BARLY	9/8/18		Resting + Bathing	BARLY MPPY Pistol Shell 51 s.w. 9pm
do	10/8/18	9 am	Training	9pm
do	11/8/18	10 am	Musketry & Lewis Gunnery	9pm
do	12/8/18		Training	9pm
do	16/8/18		Training at BARLY for hand & Rifle Sub-sector at BRICKFIELDS. MAP REF. S2. B+D S3. a.c. Chatagne	9pm NS Chatagne
do	17/8/18	9 am	Returned	

H.R.

Grampray Cox

Original

CONFIDENTIAL

AUGUST 1918.

Army Form C. 2118.

WAR DIARY
or
INTELLIGENCE SUMMARY.
(Erase heading not required.)

15th Bn ESSEX REGT.

Instructions regarding War Diaries and Intelligence Summaries are contained in F. S. Regs., Part II. and the Staff Manual respectively. Title pages will be prepared in manuscript.

Place	Date	Hour	Summary of Events and Information	Remarks and references to Appendices
BRICKFIELDS	18/8/18	4—	Bn — Support	6pm
do	19/8/18	—"	do	6pm
do	20/8/18 to 22/8/18	do	do	8pm
do	23/8/18	2.0—	Bn. moved by Route March to Bagnes at SAULTY, staying V & X H.3.9+q	7pm
SAULTY	24/8/18	10am	Bn— entrained at SAULTY Station & proceeded to AIRE, staying left of Station 36 A.9.32.d.	6pm
"	25/8/18	9—	Bn. moved by Route March to LA. LACQUE.	
LA LACQUE	26/8/18	9—	Bn. Battn.	
do	27/8/18	2.0.	" Entrained at LA LACQUE for ST FLORIS. MAP REF P 5+6 Sheet	5am
			relieving 10th Bn Devonshire Regt. at LALONNE 36 A.	5am
ST FLORIS	29/8/18	8.0—	" Proceeded Bn H.Q. as above. Sheet 36 A Sheet 1/5	5pm
do	28/8/18	daily	" in front line	7pm
do	29/8/18	do	— do — Advance 500' — do — at COLONNE SUR LYS	8pm
do	30/8/18	do	— do — Advance continued entered RESTREM. Bn H.Q. MERVILLE	4pm
do	31/8/18	do	— do — Crossed River LAWE & entered LA GORGUE	6pm

G. Menny Bruggl Lieut. Colonel
Comdg. 15th Bn. The Essex Regt.

WAR DIARY
INTELLIGENCE SUMMARY

Army Form C. 2118.

Sept 1918.

1st Bn Queen's Regt

Place	Date	Hour	Summary of Events and Information	Remarks and references to Appendices
MERVILLON	1/9/18		Bn in front line south of sugar at NEURILLON. Bn in attempt to regain ground. Then moved to LESTREM	
"	2/9/18		Bn relieved in front line, returned to Billets in LESTREM	
LESTREM	3/9/18		do by 25th Bn King's Liverpool Regt + moved to Billets at ST FLORIS	
ST FLORIS	4/9/18		do at Billets at ST FLORIS	
"	5/9/18		do — do — do —	
EPINETTE	6/9/18		Bn in bivouacs at ERNETTE	
"	7/9/18		do moved to Billets — LESTREM	
LESTREM	9/9/18		O — Billets LESTREM	
"	10/9/18		Bn relieved 25 Bn R W F + left for lept line of manoeuvre round bn line PONT RIQUEUL	

WAR DIARY
or
INTELLIGENCE SUMMARY.

(Erase heading not required.)

Army Form C. 2118.

Sept. 1918. 15th Royal Sussex Regt.

Place	Date	Hour	Summary of Events and Information	Remarks and references to Appendices
B36.a.9.5	10/9/18 to 12/9/18		Bn in Intro line of Reserve Brigade	9mm 5mm
do	13/9/18		Bn relieved 25th Kings trench and left in Support Reserve line south of M14a49 Keen st. M14a49	9mm
M14.d.9.9	14/9/18		Bn in Support Reserve line	9mm
	15/9/18			9mm
M14.d.9.9	16/9/18		Bn relieved 11th Bn A.I.F. left sub-sector Divisional Reserve and moved B.In. of HARLECK CASTLE	5mm
Harleck Castle	17/9/18		do	5mm
do	18/9/18		do	5mm
do	19/9/18		do	5mm

WAR DIARY
or
INTELLIGENCE SUMMARY.
(Erase heading not required.)

Army Form C. 2118.

Sept 1918.

15th Bn Essex Regt

Place	Date	Hour	Summary of Events and Information	Remarks and references to Appendices
HARLECK CASTLE	21/9/18	4.36 a.m	Raid carried out by 2 officers + 30 OR. Carried out on TWO TREE FARM, N.7.b.55.75 leaving WINDY POST at 4.36 A.M. A preliminary assault of tanks was to be met by the enemy held at N.7.d.8.7 and men went out to let our men through. The party in the centre attacked Germans in the front + cleared dugouts + about 30 men into dugouts at N.7.d.9.8 by our troops up to N7b front party to have another enemy fully attacked + advanced from dugouts up by N7b front party to the objective. Hit not met well hung up 9 OR party to attack enemy position relieved in WINDY POST was bombarded now 1 officer wounded. 1 OR killed + 4 wounded.	Ref. 3G.SWI 15.00
do	22/9/18		Bn. relieved by 36th Northumberland Fusiliers and proceeded to Dug-outs + billets at RIEZ BAILLEUL	SMM
RIEZ BAILLEUL	23/9/18		Bn. at RIEZ BAILLEUL	SMM

S.M.Murphy Lt Col
comdg 15th Essex Regt

Army Form C. 2118.

WAR DIARY
or
INTELLIGENCE SUMMARY. Sept 1918

(Erase heading not required.)

Place	Date	Hour	Summary of Events and Information	Remarks and references to Appendices
RIEZ BAILLEUL	24/9/18 to 27/9/18		Bn at RIEZ BAILLEUL	8pm
do	28/9/18		do	8pm
do	30/9/18		Bn relieved 11th Bn Royal Scots Battalion in front line near Det at M17 c 46. Refs 36.SW1	8pm

E.J. Murphy Major
Comdg 15th Bn Northum. Reg.

CONFIDENTIAL

WAR DIARY
or
INTELLIGENCE SUMMARY.
(Erase heading not required.)

Army Form C. 2118.

October 1916
15TH BN ESSEX REGT.

Place	Date	Hour	Summary of Events and Information	Remarks and references to Appendices
FAUQUISSART	1/10/16		Bn in Front line at MASSELOT TRENCH. Map Sheet 36 SW	8mm
do	2/10/16		Bn relieved by London Scot Regt. & moved to billets in LA BASSE ROAD	8mm
LA BASSE ROAD	3/10/16		AM moved to LAVENTIE NORTH POST.	8mm
LAVENTIE N. POST	4/10/16		do at LAVENTIE	8mm
do	5/10/16		Bn moved to CROIX MARECHAL	8mm
CROIX MARECHAL	6/10/16		Bn Relieved 16. D.L.I. in front line	8mm
Front line	7/10/16		Bn — Front line	8mm
do	8/10/16		do	8mm
do	9/10/16		do	8mm
do	10/10/16		Bn relieved by 30 N.F. and moved to billets at Fleurbaix	8mm

61R

CONFIDENTIAL (2)

Army Form C. 2118.

WAR DIARY October 1918

or

INTELLIGENCE SUMMARY. 15th ESSEX REGT.

(Erase heading not required.)

Continued from Sheet I

Place	Date	Hour	Summary of Events and Information	Remarks and references to Appendices
FLEURBAIX	1/10/18		Brigade in Divnl Reserve. — Battalion Training —	See App Sheet 36.
do	2/10/18			
do	13/10/18			
do	14/10/18			
do	15/10/18			
do	16/10/18		Bn moved to BOIS GRENIER Sheet 36.	
BOIS GRENIER	17/10/18		Bn moved to PREMESQUES do.	
PREMESQUES	18/10/18		Bn marched to capture ST. ANDRE [Sheet 36] continuing at night through LA MADELEINE to ST MAURICE [Antwerp-sur-Seine].	
ST MAURICE	19/10/18		Bn marched to LE MARAIS. [Sheet 36]	

Army Form C. 2118.

WAR DIARY
or
INTELLIGENCE SUMMARY.
(Erase heading not required.)

October 1918.

15th Bn. ESSEX REGT.

Place	Date	Hour	Summary of Events and Information	Remarks and references to Appendices
LEMARAIS	20/10/18		Bn marched to TOUFFLERS. [Billets]	8mn
TOUFFLERS	21/10/18		" at above.	8mn
do	22/10/18		Brigade relieved 176 Bde in line Batt in Brigade Reserve at HULANS. About 8.9	8mn
HULANS	23/10/18 to 25/10/18		Bn at HULANS.	8mn
do	26/10/18		Bn relieved 11th S.L.I. in Right Front Brigade Sector.	8mn
EPINETTE	27/10/18		Bn in Front line.	8mn

CONFIDENTIAL.

Army Form C. 2118.

WAR DIARY
or
~~INTELLIGENCE SUMMARY.~~

(Erase heading not required.)

October 1916

15th Bn Essex Regt

Week 3

Place	Date	Hour	Summary of Events and Information	Remarks and references to Appendices
EPINETTE	28/10/16		Bn in front line.	S.9.d....
do	29/10/16		— do —	S.9.d....
do	30/10/16		— do —	S.9.d....
do	31/10/16		— do —	S.9.d....

Signature

Lieut. O'Neil

WAR DIARY or INTELLIGENCE SUMMARY

Army Form C. 2118.

NOVEMBER 1918

15th Bn. Essex Regt.

Place	Date	Hour	Summary of Events and Information	Remarks and references to Appendices
EPINETTE H.29.a.9.9	1/11/18		Battn. in front line in right of Brigade sector. Hostile shelling active on morning & normal during day.	Sheet 37
	2/11/18	0800	Patrol consisting of 1 Sergeant and 5 men went out, but were cut off by the enemy in a loop of river Sekeute at I.26.b.0.2	Sheet 37
		1400	Enemy shelled A Coy area (H.25 & 4.9) very heavily, causing the company to move into fresh billets at CHAUNY in H.28.	do
		1930	Sergt. & three men of patrol cut off this morning returned into coys of Menkness. Sergt. wounded several times & also one man, remaining him, not kit. Bodies of two men killed had to be left on river bank and subsequently recovered.	do
		2300	Raiding party consisting of 2 Lt. Hampton & 11 O. Ranks tried entering lost at I.26.b.0.2 Party searched at 0030 having found post at I.26.b.0.2 unoccupied.	do
	3/11/18	0530	Battalion relieved by 2/6th Bn. Durham L.I. and returned to billets at HULLUCH at H.20.d	do
HULLUCH H.20.d	4/11/18		Battalion resting	do
	5/11/18		Training & recreation	do
	6/11/18	1530	Battalion relieved 11th Bn. Somerset L.I. in left out sector of 178 Bde front, with outpost company in CABARET LIETARD. Bn. HQ in Chateau at I.19.b.5.2	do
I.19.b.5.2	7/11/18		Hostile artillery and M.G's normal. Slight gas shelling.	do
do	8/11/18		Battalion relieved by 13th Bn West Riding Regt of 178 Inf Bde. Battalion moved into billets at TOUFFLERS G.23.b.	do
G.23.b				

(2) CONFIDENTIAL

Army Form C. 2118.

WAR DIARY
or
INTELLIGENCE SUMMARY.
(Erase heading not required.)

NOVEMBER 1918

15th Bn ESSEX REGT

Instructions regarding War Diaries and Intelligence Summaries are contained in F. S. Regs., Part II. and the Staff Manual respectively. Title pages will be prepared in manuscript.

Place	Date	Hour	Summary of Events and Information	Remarks and references to Appendices
TOUFFLERS G23b	9/11/18		Battalion resting	Sheet 37
	10/11/18	0530	Battalion marched to GRAND REJET in J7a. to billets	do
GRAND REJET J7a	11/11/18	0930	Received order that hostilities were to cease at 11 a.m. Battalion at once marched back to HULLANS H20d.	do
HULLANS H20d	12/11/18		Battalion resting	do
	13/11/18		Battalion on Recreational Training	do
do	14/11/18		do	do
do	15/11/18		Battalion marched to GRUSON in M33b. Headquarters in Chateau in M33b05	do
GRUSON M33b	16/11/18		Battalion marched to SECLIN in V30a. Headquarters at V30a51	Sheet 36
SECLIN V30a	17/11/18		Battalion resting	do
do	18/11/18		Battalion training recreation. Reinforcements 34 o/ranks from base	do
do	19/11/18		do	do
do	20/11/18		do 50 o/ranks from base	do
do	21/11/18		Education scheme commenced Coy. Elementary classes opened	do
do	22/11/18		Battalion training recreation. Education classes open	do
do	23/11/18		do	do

Page 3.

CONFIDENTIAL

Army Form C. 2118.

WAR DIARY
or
INTELLIGENCE SUMMARY.

NOVEMBER 1918

15TH Bn ESSEX REGT

(Erase heading not required.)

Place	Date	Hour	Summary of Events and Information	Remarks and references to Appendices
SECLIN	24/11/18		Brigade Church Parade.	Sheet 36
V30a	25/11/18		Battalion training, education, recreation.	do
do	26/11/18		do — do —	do
do	27/11/18		do — do —	do
do	28/11/18		Advance billetting party of 1 Offr and 4 o/ranks proceeded to NOEUX-LES-MINES. Usual training	do
do	29/11/18		Battalion training, education, recreation	do
do	30/11/18		do	

CONFIDENTIAL

Army Form C. 2118.

WAR DIARY
or
INTELLIGENCE SUMMARY.

(Erase heading not required.)

DECEMBER 1918

15TH BN Essex Regt

Place	Date	Hour	Summary of Events and Information	Remarks and references to Appendices
SECLIN V30a	1/12/18	0930	Battalion Church Parade	Sheet 36
	2/12/18	0900	Brigade Field Day	do
		1400	Recreational Training	do
do	3/12/18	—	Battalion Training, Educational classes recreational training	do
do	4/12/18	—	do	do
	5/12/18	0900	Battalion moved by lorries to NOEUX-LES-MINES (K18 b+d) Headquarters at L19 a 3.5 Sheet B	44
		1400	Cleaning billets etc	1/40,000
NOEUX-LES-MINES K18 b+d	6/12/18	—	Battalion on Interior Economy, Cleaning billets, recreational training	do
do	7/12/18	—	Battalion training, Education classes recreational training	do
do	8/12/18	0930	Battalion on Brigade Church Parade	do
do	9/12/18	—	Battalion training, Educational classes & recreational training	do
do	10/12/18	—	do	do
do	11/12/18	—	Proceeded to England for dispersal — two colminers	do
			Battalion training Educational classes recreational training 12 [pester coal miners] sent to England for dispersal	do
do	12/12/18	—	Battalion Route march (L13C1.9 – L3b4.4 – L17b3.8 – L22 d3.6 – L13C1.9) Recreation	do
			40 reinforcements joined the battalion from Base Depot	

G. Moore Major
15th Essex

CONFIDENTIAL
Page 2

WAR DIARY or INTELLIGENCE SUMMARY.

Army Form C. 2118.

DECEMBER 1918

10th Bn. The Essex Regt.

Place	Date	Hour	Summary of Events and Information	Remarks and references to Appendices
NEUX-LES-MINES K18 b+d	13/12/18	—	Battalion bathing, training, Educational classes + Recreational Training	Sheet
	14/12/18	—	Battalion training, Educational classes, Recreational Training	w.o.
do	15/12/18	—	Battn. Church Parade in YMCA Hut, NEUX-LES-MINES	do
do	16/12/18	—	Battn. Training, Educational classes, Recreational Training	do
do	17/12/18	—	Battalion training, bathing, Educational Classes, Recreational Training	do
do	18/12/18	—	do	do
do	19/12/18	—	do	do
do	20/12/18	—	Battalion Route march (L13 C19 – L3 b4 + – L17 b 3.8 – L22 d8.6 – L17 C1.9) Recreation	do
do	21/12/18	—	Battalion Training, Education classes, Recreation	do
do	22/12/18	1200	do	do
do	23/12/18	—	Battalion Church Parade. Service in YMCA Hut NEUX-LES-MINES	do
do	24/12/18	—	Battalion Training, Education, Salvage + Camp construction + Recreation	do
do	25/12/18	—	do — Xmas in Trenches, Recreation	do
do	26/12/18	—	Christmas Day observed as a holiday, Voluntary Services	do
do	27/12/18	—	Observed as a holiday	do
do	28/12/18	—	Battalion Training, Education, Salvage Camp Construction, Recreation	do
do	29/12/18	11.45	do — Hut Cleaning, fatigues etc	do
do	30/12/18	—	Battalion Church Parade. Service in YMCA Hut	do
do	31/12/18	—	Battalion Training, Education classes, Salvage Camp Construction, Recreation	do
do			Battalion Training, bathing, Education classes, Salvage etc Recreation	do

Lieut. C. Lorch

CONFIDENTIAL

WAR DIARY
INTELLIGENCE SUMMARY.

(Erase heading not required.)

JANUARY 1919

15TH BN ESSEX REGT

Army Form C. 2118.

Instructions regarding War Diaries and Intelligence Summaries are contained in F. S. Regs., Part II. and the Staff Manual respectively. Title pages will be prepared in manuscript.

Place	Date	Hour	Summary of Events and Information	Remarks and references to Appendices
NEUX-LES-MINES. K24 6.8.7	1/1/19	0900	Battalion firing on Range at K29a 5.5. Platoon Competition.	Sheet 36
	2/1/19	—	Battalion training, Education classes & Salvage. Recreation	do
do	3/1/19	—	do Lecture on "Citizenship" by Educ. Officer.	do
do	4/1/19	—	do Salvage. Recreation	do
do	5/1/19	—	Voluntary Services in YMCA Hut.	do
do	6/1/19	—	Battalion Training, Education classes and Salvage. Recreation	do
do	7/1/19	—	do do	do
do	8/1/19	—	do Lecture on Citizenship by Educ. Officer. Recreation	do
do	9/1/19	—	do Salvage & Camp Construction. Recreation	do
do	10/1/19	—	Battalion Route March. K24 a 6.6 – K27 a 9.2 – K19 a 5.1 – K15 c 3.5 – K18 d 3.7 – K24 a 6.6 Recreation	do
do	11/1/19	—	Battalion Training, Education classes & Salvage. Recreation	do
do	12/1/19	1100	Parade Service in YMCA Hut. Voluntary services.	do
do	13/1/19	—	Battalion firing on range at K29 a 5.5. Platoon Competition	do
do	14/1/19	1600	Battalion entrained at NEUX-LES-MINES for DIEPPE area	do
do	15/1/19	—	Battalion on journey to DIEPPE area	Sheet DIEPPE
MARTIN EGLISE	16/1/19	0300	Battalion arrived at ROUXMESNIL Station	do
do	17/1/19	0700	Battalion marched to Hutted camp at MARTIN EGLISE	do
do	18/1/19	—	Battalion takes over Demobilization Camp duties from 2nd Worcester Regt.	do
do	19/1/19	—	Battalion engaged in Demobilization camp duties	do
do	20/1/19	—	do	do
do	21/1/19	—	do	do

Rehearsal of Bramley young Colours

G.R.

CONFIDENTIAL

JANUARY 1919

15th Bn Essex Regt

Army Form C. 2118.

WAR DIARY
INTELLIGENCE SUMMARY.
(Erase heading not required.)

Instructions regarding War Diaries and Intelligence Summaries are contained in F. S. Regs., Part II. and the Staff Manual respectively. Title pages will be prepared in manuscript.

Place	Date	Hour	Summary of Events and Information	Remarks and references to Appendices
MARTIN EGLISE	21/1/19	—	Battalion engaged on Demobilization Camp duties	
do	22/1/19	—	do	
do	23/1/19	1030	Battalion presented with Kings Colour by Major General WM Long a Mr. CB. Battalion marched past, and then one company escorted Colours to General's room	
do	24/1/19	—	Battalion engaged on Demobilization Camp duties	
do	25/1/19	—	do	
do	—	—	for demobilization	
do	26/1/19	—	Battalion engaged on Demobilization Camp Duties – Church parade by conference	
do	27/1/19	—	do	23 men left Battalion for
do	—	—	demobilization	
do	28/1/19	—	Battalion engaged on Demobilization Camp Duties	
do	29/1/19	—	do	
do	30/1/19	—	do	
do	31/1/19	—	do	28 men left Battalion for demobilization

G.D.Winnifrith
Lieut. Colonel
Comdg 15th Bn. The Essex Regt

WAR DIARY / INTELLIGENCE SUMMARY

(Erase heading not required.)

Army Form C. 2118.

Lostdid? February '19. 5th Bn Essex Regt

April 10

Place	Date	Hour	Summary of Events and Information	Remarks and references to Appendices
Lostdid?	1st		Brief Report on Port duties	
do	2nd		do	nil
do	3rd		do	nil
do	4th		do	nil
do	5th		do	nil
do	6th		do	nil
do	7th		do 3rd hlCo. moves off for Recoubé	nil
do	8th		do 26 Officers 23 hlCo. moves off for Recoubé	nil
do	9th		do 6th hlCo. moves off for Recoubé	nil
do	10th		do 23 hlCo. moves off for Recoubé	nil
do	11th		do 15 hlCo. + two hlCo. of hlCo. for Recoubé	nil
do	12th		do	nil
do	13th		do	nil
do	14th		do	nil
do	15th		do	nil

S.D. Humphreys
Lt Col

Army Form C. 2118.

Sheet No 2

WAR DIARY
or
INTELLIGENCE SUMMARY.

(Erase heading not required.)

Instructions regarding War Diaries and Intelligence Summaries are contained in F. S. Regs., Part II. and the Staff Manual respectively. Title pages will be prepared in manuscript.

Place	Date	Hour	Summary of Events and Information	Remarks and references to Appendices
Egypt	16		Battalion Engaged on Demobilization. Struck Parade by Companies. Sent to Base 2 Officers 211 O.R.'s.	Sheet 1. Sm
	17		do	Sm
	18		do	Sm
	19		do	Sm
	20		do 7 h.L.G. + 1 Lewis gun belt for Demob.	Sm
	21		do	Sm
	22		do	Sm
	23		do Church Parade by Companies	Sm
	24		do	Sm
	25		do 36 h.L.G. + 1m Gyr B.a.r. for Demob.	Sm
	26		Battalion moved to Kalais. Relieved of Demobilization by 9/B Royal Fusiliers.	Sm
Calais	27		Battalion arrived at No 5 Camp Kalais	Sm
	28		Battalion took over No 6 Camp having arrived at Calais from 4 Cambrai Railway.	Sm

Monroppe

WAR DIARY

OF

15TH BATTALION ESSEX REGIMENT

FOR

MARCH, 1919.

WAR DIARY
INTELLIGENCE SUMMARY.
(Erase heading not required.)

Army Form C. 2118.

March, 1919

15th Bn. Essex Regiment

Place	Date	Hour	Summary of Events and Information	Remarks and references to Appendices
Calais	1.3.19		Battalion engaged on Camp duties in No. 8 Leave Camp & Guards in Calais Area.	8mm
"	2.3.19		Battalion engaged on Camp duties in No. 8 Leave Camp & Guards in Calais Area. Church Parade by Companies.	8mm
"	3.3.19		Battalion engaged on Camp duties in No. 8 Leave Camp & Guards in Calais Area.	8mm
"	4.3.19		Battalion engaged on Camp duties in No. 8 Leave Camp & Guards in Calais Area.	8mm
"	5.3.19		— do —	8mm
"	6.3.19		— do —	8mm
"	7.3.19		— do —	8mm
"	8.3.19		— do —	8mm
"	9.3.19		— do — Church parade by Companies.	8mm

Army Form C. 2118.

WAR DIARY
INTELLIGENCE SUMMARY.
(Erase heading not required.)

1st Bn. Essex Regiment

Place	Date	Hour	Summary of Events and Information	Remarks and references to Appendices
Calais	10/3/19		Battalion engaged on Camp duties in Calais area.	8 a.m.
"	11/3/19		— do. —	8 a.m.
"	12/3/19		— do. —	8 a.m.
"	13/3/19		— do. —	8 a.m.
"	14/3/19		— do. —	6 a.m.
"	15/3/19		— do. —	8 a.m.
"	16/3/19		Battalion engaged on Camp duties in No. 6 Leave Camp. Church Parade by Companies.	8 a.m.
"	17/3/19		Battalion engaged on Camp duties in Calais Area.	8 a.m.
"	18/3/19		— do. —	8 a.m.
"	19/3/19		— do. —	8 a.m.
"	20/3/19		Battalion engaged on Camp duties in Nos. 5 & 6 Leave Camps & Guards in Calais Area. 1 Officer and 32 other ranks to Dispersal Station for demobilization.	8 a.m.

WAR DIARY
or
INTELLIGENCE SUMMARY.

(Erase heading not required.)

Army Form C. 2118.

15th Bn. Essex Regiment

Place	Date	Hour	Summary of Events and Information	Remarks and references to Appendices
Calais	21/3/19		Battalion engaged on Camp duties in Nos. 5 & 8 Leave Camps in Calais Area.	
"	22/3/19		— do. — 20 other ranks to dispersal station for demobilization.	
"	23/3/19		Battalion engaged on Camp duties in Nos. 6 & 8 Leave Camps in Calais Area. Church Parade by Companies.	
"	24/3/19		Battalion engaged on Camp duties in Nos. 5 & 8 Leave Camps in Calais area. 15 other ranks to dispersal station for demobilization.	
"	25/3/19		Battalion engaged on Camp duties in Nos. 5 & 8 Leave Camps & Guards in Calais Area.	
"	26/3/19		— do. —	
"	27/3/19		— do. —	
"	28/3/19		Battalion engaged on Camp duties in Nos. 5 & 8 Leave Camps & Guards in Calais Area. 3 Officers and 11 other ranks to dispersal Station for demobilization. Lecture by Commanding Officer.	

WAR DIARY
or
INTELLIGENCE SUMMARY.
(Erase heading not required.)

Army Form C. 2118.

15th Bn. Essex Regiment

Place	Date	Hour	Summary of Events and Information	Remarks and references to Appendices
Calais	29/3/19		Battalion engaged on Camp duties in Nos. 5 & 8 Leave Camps & Guards in Calais Area. Lecture by Commanding Officer.	
"	30/3/19		do. do. & Church Parade by Coy.	
"	31/3/19		Battalion engaged on Camp duties in Nos. 5 & 8 Leave Camps & Guards in Calais Area. Close order drill by Sections & Platoon & rifle Physical Training & Lecture by Commanding Officer.	

(Stanley Wright)
Lieut. Col.
Commanding 15th Bn. Essex Regt.

Confidential.

WAR DIARY

OF

15TH BATTN. ESSEX REGIMENT

FOR

APRIL, 1919.

Army Form C. 2118.

Sheet 1

15th ESSEX R.

WAR DIARY
or
INTELLIGENCE SUMMARY.
(Erase heading not required.)

April 1919

Place	Date	Hour	Summary of Events and Information	Remarks and references to Appendices
CALAIS	APRIL 1st		Battalion engaged on Camp duties in Nos. 5 & 8 Leave Camps, Grounds in Calais Area and General Training. 14 other ranks proceeded to Dispersal Station for demobilization.	RRNL
do.	2nd		Battalion engaged on Camp duties in Nos. 5 & 8 Leave Camps, Grounds in Calais Area and General Training. 1 other rank proceeded to Dispersal Station for demobilization.	RRNL
do.	3rd		Battalion engaged on Camp duties in Nos. 5 & 8 Leave Camps, Grounds in Calais Area and General Training. 2 other ranks proceeded to Dispersal Station for demobilization.	RRNL
do.	4th		Battalion engaged on Camp duties in Nos. 5 & 8 Leave Camps, Grounds in Calais Area and General Training. 1 Officer & 2 other ranks proceeded to Dispersal Station for demobilization.	RRNL
do.	5th		Battalion engaged on Camp duties in Nos. 5 & 8 Leave Camps, Grounds in Calais Area and General Training. 6 other ranks proceeded to Dispersal Station for demobilization.	RRNL

Army Form C. 2118.

15th ESSEX R. WAR DIARY or INTELLIGENCE SUMMARY.

(Erase heading not required.)

APRIL 1919

Place	Date	Hour	Summary of Events and Information	Remarks and references to Appendices
CALAIS	APRIL 6th		Battalion engaged on Camp duties in Nos. 5 & 8 Leave Camps, and Guards in Calais Area. Church Parade by Battalion. 2 Officers & 15 other ranks joined from 9th Bn. Essex Regiment.	RRK
do.	7th		Battalion engaged on Camp duties in Nos. 5 & 8 Leave Camps, Guards in Calais Area and General Training. 1 other rank proceeded to Infernal Station for demobilization.	RRK
do.	8th		Battalion engaged on Camp duties in Nos. 5 & 8 Leave Camps, Guards in Calais Area, and General Training. 2 other ranks proceeded to Infernal Station for demobilization.	RRK
do.	9th		Battalion engaged on Camp duties in Nos. 5 & 8 Leave Camps, Guards in Calais Area and General Training.	RRK
do.	10th		Battalion engaged on Camp duties in Nos. 5 & 8 Leave Camps, Guards in Calais Area, and General Training. 2 Officers and 1 other rank proceeded to Infernal Station for demobilization.	RRK
do.	11th		Battalion engaged on Camp duties in Nos. 5 & 8 Leave Camps, Guards in Calais Area and General Training.	RRK

Sheet 3

15th ESSEX R.

Army Form C. 2118.

WAR DIARY
INTELLIGENCE SUMMARY

April 1919

Place	Date	Hour	Summary of Events and Information	Remarks and references to Appendices
CALAIS	APRIL 12th		Battalion engaged in Camp duties in Nos. 5 & 6 Leave Camps. Guards in Calais Area and General Training.	RRM/r
do.	13th		Battalion engaged on Camp duties in Nos. 5 & 6 Leave Camps and Guards in Calais Area. Church Parade by Companies.	RRM/r
do.	14th		Battalion engaged on Camp duties in Nos. 5 & 6 Leave Camps. Guards in Calais Area & General Training. The Commanding Officer (Lieut. Col. E. J. Hornby-Knight) and Capt. R.W. Stapley proceeded to England for demobilization. 3 other ranks proceed to Dieppe Station for demobilization.	RRM/r
do.	15th		Battalion engaged on Camp duties in Nos. 5 & 6 Leave Camps. Guards in Calais Area and General Training. One officer (Lieut. R. Bigford) joined from 9th Essex Regt.	RRM/r
do.	16th		Battalion engaged on Camp duties in Nos. 5 & 6 Leave Camps. Guards in Calais Area and General Training. One officer proceeded to Dieppe Station for demobilization.	RRM/r

Army Form C. 2118.

15th ESSEX R.

WAR DIARY
INTELLIGENCE SUMMARY

(Erase heading not required.)

April 1919

Place	Date	Hour	Summary of Events and Information	Remarks and references to Appendices
CALAIS	April 17th		Battalion engaged on Camp duties in Nos. 5 & 6 Leave Camps in Calais Area & general training. 9 other ranks joined from 9th Bn. Essex Regt. Lieut. Col. A.E. Maitland DSO M.C. assumed command of the Battalion from to-day.	
do.	18th (Good Friday)		Battalion engaged on Camp duties in Nos. 5 & 8 Leave Camps & numbers in Calais Area. Church Parade by Companies.	RM/1. RM/2.
do.	19th.		Battalion engaged on Camp duties in Nos. 5 & 8 Leave Camps & numbers in Calais Area. To training parades.	RM/3.
do.	20th		Battalion engaged on Camp duties in Nos. 5 & 8 Leave Camps & numbers in Calais Area. Church Parade by Companies.	RM/4.
do.	21st (Easter Monday)		Battalion engaged on Camp duties in Nos. 5 & 8 Leave Camps & numbers in Calais Area. To training parades. 5 other ranks proceeded to England, Scotland for demobilization.	RM/5.
do.	22nd		Battalion engaged on Camp duties in Nos. 5 & 8 Leave Camps & numbers in Calais Area & general training.	RM/6.

Sheet 5

WAR DIARY

INTELLIGENCE SUMMARY

15th ESSEX R.

April 1919

Army Form C. 2118.

Place	Date	Hour	Summary of Events and Information	Remarks and references to Appendices
CALAIS	April 23rd		Battalion engaged on Camp duties in Nos. 5 & 6 Leave Camps, Guards in Calais Area & General Training.	RRN Lt
do.	24th		Battalion engaged on Camp duties in Nos. 5 & 6 Leave Camps, Guards in Calais Area & General Training.	RRN Lt
do.	25th		Battalion engaged on Camp duties in Nos. 5 & 6 Leave Camps, Guards in Calais Area, General Training, & other ranks proceeded to Boulogne Station for demobilization.	RRN Lt
do.	26th		Battalion engaged on Camp duties in Nos. 5 & 6 Leave Camps, Guards in Calais Area with general training, 1 other rank proceeded to Boulogne Station for demobilization.	RRN Lt
do.	27th		Battalion engaged on Camp duties in Nos. 5 & 6 Leave Camps, Guards in Calais Area & other ranks proceeded to Boulogne Station for demobilization. (Church Parade by Battalion)	RRN Lt
do.	28th		Battalion engaged on Camp duties in Nos. 5 & 6 Leave Camps, Guards in Calais Area & General Training.	RRN Lt

Army Form C. 2118.

15th ESSEX R

WAR DIARY
INTELLIGENCE SUMMARY.
(Erase heading not required.)

April 1918

Place	Date	Hour	Summary of Events and Information	Remarks and references to Appendices
CALAIS	APRIL 29th		Battalion engaged on Camp duties in Nos 5 & 8 Leave Camps, General in Calais Area, and General Training.	RAP/-
do	30th		Battalion engaged on Camp duties in Nos 5 & 8 Leave Camps in Calais Area and General Training. One other rank transferred to Hospital Station for investigation.	RAP/-

William Nigren
Lieut Col
Commanding 15th Bn. Essex Regiment.

CONFIDENTIAL.

WAR DIARY

OF

15TH BATTN. ESSEX REGIMENT

FOR

MAY, 1919.

WAR DIARY
INTELLIGENCE SUMMARY
(Erase heading not required.)

Army Form C. 2118.

Place	Date	Hour	Summary of Events and Information	Remarks and references to Appendices
Calais	MAY 1st		Battalion engaged on Camp duties in Nos. 5 & 8 Leave Camps, Guards in Calais Area, and General Training.	RNL.
do.	2nd		Battalion engaged on Camp duties in Nos. 5 & 8 Leave Camps, Guards in Calais Area, and General Training. 4 other ranks proceeded to Divisional School for Anti-Gas instruction.	RNL.
do.	3rd		Battalion engaged on Camp duties in Nos. 5 & 8 Leave Camps, Guards in Calais Area, and General Training. 1 other rank proceeded to Divisional School for Anti-Gas instruction.	RNL.
do.	4th		Battalion engaged on Camp duties in Nos. 5 & 8 Leave Camps, Guards in Calais Area and Church Parade by Coys.	RNL.
do.	5th		Battalion engaged on Camp duties in Nos. 5 & 8 Leave Camps, Guards in Calais Area, and General Training.	RNL.
do.	6th		Battalion engaged on Camp duties in Nos. 5 & 8 Leave Camps, Guards in Calais Area and General Training.	RNL.

Army Form C. 2118.

WAR DIARY
or
INTELLIGENCE SUMMARY.
(Erase heading not required.)

Instructions regarding War Diaries and Intelligence Summaries are contained in F. S. Regs., Part II. and the Staff Manual respectively. Title pages will be prepared in manuscript.

Place	Date	Hour	Summary of Events and Information	Remarks and references to Appendices
Calais	7th		Battalion engaged on Camp Duties in No. 5 & 6 Leave Camps, Guards in Calais Area and General Training. 3 other ranks proceeded to Dispersal Station for demobilization. Major Rea P/Regt. assumes duties of Sergeant in Command of Battalion.	
do	8th		Battalion employed on Camp Duties in Nos. 5 & 6 Leave Camps, Guards in Calais Area and General Training. 12 other ranks proceeded to Dispersal Station for demobilization.	RM L.
do	9th		Battalion engaged on Camp Duties in Nos. 5 & 6 Leave Camps, Guards in Calais Area and General Training. 1 other rank proceeded to Dispersal Station for demobilization.	RM L.
do	10th		Battalion employed on Camp Duties in Nos. 5 & 6 Leave Camps, Guards in Calais Area and General Training. 3 Lieutenants & Subalterns to Dispersal Station for demobilization.	RM L.
do	11th		Battalion engaged on Camp Duties in Nos. 5 & 6 Leave Camps, Guards in Calais Area and Church Parade by Coys.	RM L.

Army Form C. 2118.

WAR DIARY
or
INTELLIGENCE SUMMARY.
(Erase heading not required.)

Place	Date	Hour	Summary of Events and Information	Remarks and references to Appendices
Calais	12th		Battalion engaged on Camp duties in Nos. 5 & 6 Leave Camps, Generally in Calais Area and General Training.	RML.
do	13th		Battalion engaged on Camp duties in Nos. 5 & 6 Leave Camps, Generally in Calais Area and General Training. 14 other ranks proceeded to Reported Sick for Hospitalization.	RML.
do	14th		Battalion engaged on Camp duties in Nos. 5 & 6 Leave Camps, Generally in Calais Area, and General Training.	RML.
do	15th		Battalion engaged on Camp duties in Nos. 5 & 6 Leave Camps, Generally in Calais Area and General Training. 61 other ranks proceeded to Dispersal Station for hospitalization.	RML.
do	16th		Battalion engaged on Camp duties in Nos. 5 & 6 Leave Camps, Generally in Calais Area and General Training.	RML.
do	17th		Battalion engaged on Camp duties in Nos. 5 & 6 Leave Camps, Generally in Calais Area and General Training. 3 other ranks proceeded to Dispersal Station for hospitalization.	RML.

Army Form C. 2118.

WAR DIARY
or
INTELLIGENCE SUMMARY.
(Erase heading not required.)

Instructions regarding War Diaries and Intelligence Summaries are contained in F. S. Regs., Part II, and the Staff Manual respectively. Title pages will be prepared in manuscript.

Place	Date	Hour	Summary of Events and Information	Remarks and references to Appendices
Calais	18th		Battalion engaged on Camp duties in Nos 5 & 8 Leave Camps, Grounds in Calais Area and Church Parade by Coys.	RRNL.
do	19th		Battalion engaged on Camp duties in Nos 5 & 8 Leave Camps, Grounds in Calais Area and General Training.	RRNL.
do	20th		Battalion engaged on Camp duties in Nos 5 & 6 Leave Camps, Grounds in Calais Area and General Training.	RRNL.
do	21st		Battalion engaged on Camp duties in Nos 5 & 8 Leave Camps, Grounds in Calais Area and General Training. 1 Other rank proceeded to Dispersal Station for demobilisation.	RRNL.
do	22nd		Battalion engaged on Camp duties in Nos 5 & 8 Leave Camps, Grounds in Calais Area and General Training.	RRNL.
do	23rd		Battalion engaged on Camp duties in Nos 5 & 8 Leave Camps, Grounds in Calais Area and General Training.	RRNL.
do	24th		Battalion engaged on Camp duties in Nos 5 & 8 Leave Camps, Grounds in Calais Area and General Training.	RRNL.

Army Form C. 2118.

WAR DIARY
or
INTELLIGENCE SUMMARY.
(Erase heading not required.)

Instructions regarding War Diaries and Intelligence Summaries are contained in F. S. Regs., Part II. and the Staff Manual respectively. Title pages will be prepared in manuscript.

Place	Date	Hour	Summary of Events and Information	Remarks and references to Appendices
Calais	25th		Battalion engaged on Church duties in Nos 5 & 6 Leave Camps & escorts in Calais Area and Church Parade by Cups. I.O.R. proceeded to Archeul Station for demobilization.	RRM¹
do	26th		Battalion engaged on Camp duties in Nos 5 & 6 Leave Camps. Escorts in Calais Area and General Training.	RRM¹
do	27th		Battalion engaged on Camp duties in Nos 5 & 6 Leave Camps. Escorts in Calais Area and General Training.	RRM¹
do	28th		Battalion engaged on Camp duties in Nos 5 & 6 Leave Camps. Escorts in Calais Area and General Training. I.O.R. proceeded to Archeul Station for demobilization.	RRM¹
do	29th		Battalion engaged on Camp duties in Nos 5 & 6 Leave Camps. Escorts in Calais Area and General Training. I.O.R. proceeded to Archeul Station for demobilization	RRM¹
do	30th		Battalion engaged on Camp duties in Nos 5 & 6 Leave Camps. Escorts in Calais Area and General Training. I.O.R. proceeded to Archeul Station for demobilization.	RRM¹

Army Form C. 2118.

WAR DIARY
or
INTELLIGENCE SUMMARY.
(Erase heading not required.)

Place	Date	Hour	Summary of Events and Information	Remarks and references to Appendices
Calais	3/08		Battalion engaged on Camp duties in huts 578 Lines Camp, Guards in Calais Area and General Training & OR proceeded to Dispersal Station for demobilization.	RRN/1

H.A. Pollok
Major
Commanding 15th Bn Essex Regt

CONFIDENTIAL.

WAR DIARY

OF

15TH BATTN. ESSEX REGIMENT.

FOR

JUNE, 1919.

Army Form C. 2118.

WAR DIARY
or
INTELLIGENCE SUMMARY.
(Erase heading not required.)

Place	Date	Hour	Summary of Events and Information	Remarks and references to Appendices
Calais	JUNE 1st		Battalion engaged on Camp Duties in Nos 5 & 8 Leave Camps. Church Parade	
"	2nd		Guards in Calais Area & General Training } by Coys	RRMl.
"	3rd		do.	
"	4th		do.	
"	5th		do.	RRMl.
"	6th		do.	
"	7th		do.	
"	8th		do. Church Parade by Coys.	
"	9th		Whitsun Monday. General Holiday.	RRMl.
"	10th		Battalion engaged on Camp Duties in Nos 5 & 8 Leave Camps	RRMl.
"	11th		Guards in Calais Area & General Training	
"	12th		do	RRMl.
"	13th		do	
"	14th		do	

WAR DIARY
or
INTELLIGENCE SUMMARY.

(Erase heading not required.)

Army Form C. 2118.

Place	Date	Hour	Summary of Events and Information	Remarks and references to Appendices
Calais	15th		Battalion engaged on Camp duties in Nos. 5 & 6 Leave Camps & Church Pde by Coy	RRNL
"	16th		Guards in Calais Area, & general Training	
"	17th		do.	
"	18th		do.	
"	19th		do.	RRNL
"	20th		do.	
"	21st		do.	
"	22nd		do.	Church Parade by Coy	RRNL
"	23rd		do.	Hours received not Germany	
"			order to sign Peace terms.	RRNL
"	24th		General Holiday in view of above.	RRNL
"	25th		Battalion engaged on Camp duties in Nos. 5 & 6 Leave Camps	
"			Guards in Calais Area & general Training	RRNL
"	26th		do.	
"	27th		do.	RRNL

Army Form C. 2118.

WAR DIARY
or
INTELLIGENCE SUMMARY.
(Erase heading not required.)

Place	Date	Hour	Summary of Events and Information	Remarks and references to Appendices
Calais	28th		Battalion engaged on Guard Duties in the S.O.S. Leave Camps, Generals Area throughout. "PEACE SIGNED"	RRM.
"	29th		do. Church Parade by Coys + 2/6th Durham Light Infantry	RRM.
"	30th		Exchange of duties with 2/6th Durham Light Infantry. Nos. 6 + 7 Camps.	RRM.

W. Moorhouse
Lieut. Col.
Commanding 1st Bn Essex Regt.

CONFIDENTIAL.

WAR DIARY

OF

15TH BATTN. ESSEX REGIMENT

FOR

JULY, 1919.

Army Form C. 2118.

WAR DIARY
INTELLIGENCE SUMMARY.
(Erase heading not required.)

Instructions regarding War Diaries and Intelligence
Summaries are contained in F. S. Regs., Part II.
and the Staff Manual respectively. Title pages
will be prepared in manuscript.

Place	Date	Hour	Summary of Events and Information	Remarks and references to Appendices
Calais	JULY 1st		Battalion engaged on Camp duties in Calais Area + General Training	
	2nd		Battalion engaged on Camp duties in No. 6 Camp. Guards in Calais area + General Training	
	3rd		do.	
	4th		do.	
	5th		do.	
	6th		do.	
	7th		do. Massed Church Parade	
	8th		Battalion engaged on Camp. duties in No 6 Camp. Guards under etc Shore Groups in Calais Area. General Training.	
	9th		do.	
	10th		do.	
	11th		do.	
	12th		do.	
	13th		do. Church Parade by Cos.	

Army Form C. 2118.

WAR DIARY
— or —
INTELLIGENCE SUMMARY.
(Erase heading not required.)

Place	Date	Hour	Summary of Events and Information	Remarks and references to Appendices
Cairo	14th		General Holiday - Xmas Celebrations.	
	15th		Battalion engaged on Coy training in No. 6 Camp Grounds in Cairo from General training.	
	16th		do.	
	17th		do.	
	18th		do.	
	19th		General Holiday - Xmas Celebrations.	
	20th		Battalion engaged on Coy training in No. 6 Camp Grounds in Cairo also Church Parade by Coys.	
	21st		do. General training.	
	22nd		do.	
	23rd		do.	
	24th		do.	
	25th		do.	

Army Form C. 2118.

WAR DIARY
or
INTELLIGENCE SUMMARY
(Erase heading not required.)

Instructions regarding War Diaries and Intelligence Summaries are contained in F. S. Regs., Part II. and the Staff Manual respectively. Title pages will be prepared in manuscript.

Place	Date	Hour	Summary of Events and Information	Remarks and references to Appendices
Calais	26th		Battalion engaged on Camp duties in No 6 Camp Grounds in Calais Area and General Training	
	27th		do & Church Parade by Coys.	
	28th		do & General Training	
	29th		do	
	30th		do	
	31st		do	

Comdg 12th Bn. The Buffs(E.K.R.)

CONFIDENTIAL.

WAR DIARY

OF

15TH BATTN. ESSEX REGT.

FOR

AUGUST, 1919.

Army Form C. 2118.

WAR DIARY
or
INTELLIGENCE SUMMARY.
(Erase heading not required.)

Instructions regarding War Diaries and Intelligence Summaries are contained in F. S. Regs., Part II. and the Staff Manual respectively. Title pages will be prepared in manuscript.

Place	Date	Hour	Summary of Events and Information	Remarks and references to Appendices
Calais	Aug 1st		Battalion engaged in Camp Duties in No 6 Camp. Guards in Calais Area & General Training	F.
	2nd		do.	F.
	3rd		do. and Church Parade by Coys.	F.
	4th		Battalion engaged in Camp Duties in No 6 Camp. Guards in Calais Area	F.
	5th		do	F.
	6th		do	F.
	7th		do	F.
	8th		do	F.
	9th		do	F.
	10th		do and Church Parade by Coys	F.
	11th		Battalion engaged in Camp Duties in No 6 Camp. Guards in Calais Area. General Training	F.
	12th		do	F.
	13th		do	F.

Army Form C. 2118.

WAR DIARY
or
INTELLIGENCE SUMMARY
(Erase heading not required.)

Instructions regarding War Diaries and Intelligence Summaries are contained in F. S. Regs., Part II. and the Staff Manual respectively. Title pages will be prepared in manuscript.

Place	Date	Hour	Summary of Events and Information	Remarks and references to Appendices
Calais	AUG. 14th		Battalion engaged in Camp Duties in No 6 Camp. Guards in Calais Area & General Training.	F.C.
	15th		do	F.C.
	16th		do	F.C.
	17th		Church Parade by Coys.	F.C.
	18th		Battalion engaged in Camp Duties in No 6 Camp. Guards in Calais Area. General Training.	F.C.
	19th		do	F.C.
	20th		do	F.C.
	21st		Battalion moved to Glasgow Camp Beaumarais.	F.C.
	22nd		Battalion engaged in Camp Duties General Training	F.C.
	23rd		do	F.C.
	24th		do Church Parade by Coys.	F.C.

Army Form C. 2118.

WAR DIARY
or
INTELLIGENCE SUMMARY.
(Erase heading not required.)

Instructions regarding War Diaries and Intelligence Summaries are contained in F. S. Regs., Part II. and the Staff Manual respectively. Title pages will be prepared in manuscript.

Place	Date	Hour	Summary of Events and Information	Remarks and references to Appendices
Beaumaris	Aug 25th		Battalion engaged in Camp Duties & General Training	
	26th		do do	
	27th		do do	
	28th		do do	
	29th		do do	
	30th		do do	
	31st		do & Church Parade by Coys.	

Signed for O.C. The Battalion

www.ingramcontent.com/pod-product-compliance
Lightning Source LLC
Chambersburg PA
CBHW081452160426
43193CB00013B/2454